LIONEL MESSI

The Unlikely Rise to Stardom of an Undersized Argentinean Kid

Roy Brandon

Lionel Messi: The Unlikely Rise to Stardom of an Undersized
Argentinean Kid

CONTENTS

CHAPTER ONE - INTRODUCING THE WORLD'S BEST 2

CHAPTER TWO - LIO, THE SMALL KID FROM ARGENTINA 6

CHAPTER THREE - THE MOVE TO SPAIN 12

CHAPTER FOUR – "LA MASIA" YOUTH ACADEMY 16

CHAPTER FIVE – THE RISE TO THE FIRST TEAM 22

CHAPTER SIX – THE HISTORIC FIRST TREBLE 30

CHAPTER SEVEN – A WELL DECORATED STAR 35

CHAPTER EIGHT – THE QUEST FOR THE WORLD CUP 45

CHAPTER NINE – MESSI OFF THE FIELD 53

CHAPTER TEN – THE KEYS TO MESSI'S SUCCESS 60

CHAPTER ELEVEN - CONCLUSIONS 70

CHAPTER ONE

INTRODUCING THE WORLD'S BEST

"You have to fight to reach your dream. You have to sacrifice and work hard for it." – Lionel Messi

IT DOESN'T SEEM LOGICAL THAT a five foot, seven inch young man from Argentina could somehow turn into the world's best soccer player. A person diagnosed with growth hormone deficiency and without the economic resources to pay for the expensive treatment to treat that condition would also not be an ideal candidate to inherit the title of "World's Best" from the likes of Diego Maradona, Ronaldo, or Pelé. But Lionel Messi defies logic and has regularly done so since he joined his first soccer team when he was only four years old.

On an almost weekly basis, Messi overwhelms his opponents, astonishes the avid soccer fan, mesmerizes the casual observer, and renders the world speechless at his relentless ability to take soccer to new levels. Quite simply, there has never been a player like Messi who could continue, week in and week out, to defy the limits of the sport and continually surprise the entire sports world. Even athletes from other sports have expressed their disbelief at Messi´s exploits on the field. NBA basketball star Kobe Bryant has said that Messi is the "greatest athlete that I´ve ever seen."

When we watch him on the field, it is easy to assume that Messi is simply a freak of nature; the lucky recipient of a God-given gift to play soccer at levels never before seen.

Carlos Tévez, Messi´s teammate on the Argentinean national team, expresses what many people feel when, speaking of Messi, says that "he is from another planet."

But is that where Lionel Messi´s talent comes from? Is he a sort of Superman, the heir of supernatural soccer abilities? Our journey into the life story of Lionel Messi will show that the Messi that captivates us on a weekly basis is the result of a life of struggle and sacrifice. We will see how an undersized boy from Argentina defied the odds and overcame numerous obstacles to become one of soccer´s most important players...of all time.

Javier Mascherano, Messi´s current Barcelona and Argentina teammate, says that "although he may not be human, it´s good that Messi still thinks he is." Lionel Messi´s modesty, shyness and quiet public demeanor spring from his own recognition of his humanity, characterized by a life of sacrifice and hard work.

In this book, we will follow Lionel Messi from his humble beginnings in a small town in Argentina, all the way to his record fifth Ballon D'or award. Though the temptation may be strong, we won't assume that Messi simply inherited a wealth of natural talent. Instead, we will retrace the path of the hard work and dedication that led him to become, hands down, the greatest player in the history of soccer.

CHAPTER TWO

LIO, THE SMALL KID FROM ARGENTINA

"In football as in watch-making, talent and elegance mean nothing without rigor and precision." – Lionel Messi

LIONEL ANDRÉS MESSI WAS BORN on June 24th in the small town of Rosario, Argentina. His father, Jorge, was a factory worker, while his mother Celia Maria worked part time cleaning houses and in a factory that made magnets. His parents were not soccer stars that taught young Lio from their own experience, but were simply modest and dedicated workers.

El Rosario is the third biggest city in Argentina and is situated along the Paraná River. Along with its many cultural centers, Rosario—like most places in Argentina—is also known for its love of soccer.

By the age of four, Lio joined his first soccer team. This team, called Grandoli, was coached by his father. After quickly learning the game and demonstrating the rare combination of natural talent, passion for the game and personal dedication, he joined a larger team called Newell´s Old Boys, also located in his hometown of Rosario.

His grandmother, Celia, was his earliest supporter, taking him to all of his games and practices while his parents worked. When she passed away around the time of Lio´s eleventh birthday, he began the custom of commemorating each goal he scored by looking up and pointing to the sky in tribute to his deceased grandmother. He continues the tradition to this day.

Lio's two older cousins, Maximiliano and Emanuel Biancucchi were also avid soccer players, and Lio benefitted from playing against them nearly every day of his youth. He was younger and much smaller than his cousins, so this daily practice allowed him to learn how to defend himself while playing against bigger and stronger opponents, and how to exploit their size and maximize the benefits of his own.

Lio played at the Newell's Old Boy soccer club from the time he was six until he was eleven years old. In very first game, his team won 6 to 0 with Lio scoring four of his team's goals. During that six year span he scored over 200 goals, averaging more than one goal per game. He was so talented and enjoyable to watch that at half time he would entertain the crowd (and his opponents) by performing ball tricks.

Lio's team at Newell's Old Boys came to be known as the "Machine of 87," due to the fact that 1987 was the year a majority of the players were born. During their time together, they were virtually unbeatable and captured numerous trophies in various tournaments both nationally and internationally, including the Friendship Cup in Peru in 1997.

Messi seemed to be on track for greatness until an unexpected turn of events changed his life. He had always been smaller than his peers, but his family and others around him thought that he eventually would have a growth spurt and catch up to the height and strength of others his age. But Lio never grew.

At age ten he was diagnosed with a growth hormone deficiency (GHD). This medical condition is caused by problems with the pituitary gland, and it's most common effect is the limitation of growth in young people. It can also cause problems in bone development, and can adversely affect the immune system. It is a treatable condition, but treatment is very expensive. The Messi family simply couldn't afford the $1,000 dollars per month expense for the medicines and other therapies needed to treat his GHD. He was only four feet, two inches tall at the time, and needed the treatment to achieve a normal height and weight for his age.

Lio's family began looking for alternatives and approached the leadership at the Newell's Old Boys soccer club to see if they could help pay for his treatment. The team's board agreed to pay the expenses, but later changed their mind. Though the club knew that Lio was a great player, they didn't want to commit to paying for the expensive treatment of such a young player who hadn't proven himself at the higher levels.

The Argentinean soccer powerhouse, River Plate had also expressed interest in having Messi join their team. As a youngster, Messi idolized Pablo Aimar, one of the best players in the country at that time who played for River Plate. Unfortunately, due to the economic collapse that Argentina suffered at the turn of the century, not even one of the wealthier soccer clubs in Argentina could afford to pay for his GHD treatment. Could this have been the end to a once promising soccer career?

CHAPTER THREE

THE MOVE TO SPAIN

"Something deep in my character allows me to take the hits and get on with trying to win." – Lionel Messi

THE MESSI FAMILY HAD RELATIVES in Spain and without any viable option to treat Messi´s GHD in their home country, they agreed to move to Barcelona to try and find a soccer club willing to take Messi in and pay for his treatment.

Once in Spain, a trial was organized with the Barcelona soccer team, one of the best soccer teams in the Spanish soccer league known as "La Liga." The director of Barcelona's first team at the time, Charlie Rexach, was so impressed with Messi's abilities that he wanted to sign him right away. At first, Barcelona was unwilling to commit to paying for his medical bills. It was uncommon for the leading major European soccer programs to commit themselves to sign foreign players of such a young age, especially players with medical conditions that could threaten their future careers.

However, Rexach was so impressed with Messi that on December 14th, 2000 Messi signed his first contract with the Barcelona soccer team. A meeting had been set up at a local restaurant, and without any paper or a computer around, his first contract was signed on the back of a paper napkin. Barcelona had agreed to sign Messi and pay for his GHD treatments as well. Messi thus became one of the youngest foreign players to sign to play with a European powerhouse soccer club.

Life wasn't easy for Lio in Barcelona at first. He had lived his whole life in El Rosario and had become accustomed to his success on the soccer field in his hometown. It wasn't easy to learn a new style of play and adopt a new lifestyle in Spain all at the same time.

On top of all that, due to a conflict between the Newell's Old Boys and the Barcelona soccer club regarding Lio's transfer, he was rarely able to play in competitions during his first year at Barcelona and was relegated to the practice squad.

After nearly a year, his mother, brothers and sister returned to Argentina while Lio stayed with his father in Barcelona. The separation of his family affected Lio and he suffered from homesickness constantly. As a timid teenager at Barcelona he kept to himself and was quiet most of the time. Some of his teammates at the Barcelona youth academy thought Lio was mute.

Despite these difficulties, Lio never gave up and continued to work hard to achieve his dreams of soccer greatness. The sacrifice of leaving family and country were one obstacle that he had to overcome in order to become the player that he is today.

CHAPTER FOUR

"LA MASIA" YOUTH ACADEMY

"My ambition is always to get better and better." – *Lionel Messi*

BARCELONA'S YOUTH ACADEMY, "LA MASIA" is famous, producing some of the world's best soccer players. It is an academy where players live and study, playing soccer around the clock.

La Masia is a Catalan world that means farmhouse in English. The facility can hold around 300 young soccer players. It has become renowned as one of the best youth football academies in the world, and in 2010, all three finalists for the FIFA Ballon D´or, soccer´s most prestigious prize for best player in the world, were trained at La Masia. That year, Lionel Messi and his teammates Xavi Hernandez and Andrés Iniesta were the final three nominees for that award. No other youth academy has had even two of the three finalists in the same year.

In today´s soccer world where players are continually transferred and the best teams are often those that are able to purchase the most expensive and talented players from around the world, Barcelona´s soccer philosophy focuses on training their own players from an early age. Louis Van Gaal, a former Barcelona coach, once dreamed of winning a Champions League trophy with a team of eleven "home-grown" players. In 2009, Barcelona won the Champions League, and of the 11 starting players, eight of them had been graduates of

La Masia youth academy. Needless to say, Messi had found his way into one of the best soccer schools in the world, one that would push him and help him unlock his true potential.

After his first year at La Masia, the contract issues were settled between Newell's Old Boys and Barcelona, so Lio was able to begin playing competitively. Some of his teammates on Barcelona's youth teams included Gerard Piqué and Cesc Fabregas, two players who would eventually be his teammates on some of Barcelona's greatest teams. One of his first coaches at Barcelona was Tita Villanova, who would coach him again years later while a member of Barcelona's first team.

Messi completed his growth hormone treatment at age 14, and though still smaller than the majority of the other players at Barcelona, he quickly established himself as one of the better players at La Masia.

He formed part of what came to be known as "The Baby Dream Team," Barcelona's greatest ever youth team. Together with Cesc Fabregas, Gerard Piqué, Pedro Rodriguez and others, they went on to win numerous trophies and establish themselves as the future of Barcelona's soccer team.

Messi quickly progressed through the ranks of Barcelona's youth academy. He played a total of 45 games for Barcelona's youth teams called "Infantil" and "Cadete." During those games he scored 59 goals, averaging more than one goal per game.

His greatest year came while playing for the "Cadetes" youth squad. He scored 36 goals in 30 games while the youth team won the infamous "Treble," winning the League Cup, the Spanish Cup, and the Catalan Cup.

In the Copa Cataluña final, Messi delivered what may be the most famous game of his youth team career. Having just suffered a broken cheekbone in practice, Messi was forced to play with a plastic mask on his face. Unaccustomed to playing with a mask, Messi took it off at halftime and quickly scored two goals within 10 minutes, before a substitution was made in order to prevent further injury to his cheek. Barcelona won the cup 4-1 and the game became known as the "Partido de la Máscara" or the "Mask Game," in English.

Barcelona was lucky to hang on to Messi. At the end of the 2002-2003 season, he was offered a contract by the English soccer team Arsenal. Messi's teammates Cesc Fabregas and Gerard Pique did leave for English clubs, but Messi decided to stay at Barcelona. Years later, Messi reminisced, saying, "Barcelona gave me everything, they took a chance on me when nobody else would. I never have any desire to play for anybody else. I will be here for as long as they want me."

Recognizing his talent, the Barcelona managers moved him up to the Barcelona C team where he scored 5 goals in 10 matches before going up to the Barcelona B team where he scored 6 goals in 22 matches.

CHAPTER FIVE

THE RISE TO THE FIRST TEAM

"The day you think there are no improvements to be made is a sad one for any player." – Lionel Messi

THE SUCCESS THAT LIO WAS HAVING at all levels of Barcelona's soccer club was evident, and it would only be a matter of time before he ascended to the first team. Finally, at sixteen years, four months and twenty three days old, Messi debuted on Barcelona's first team during a friendly match against the Portuguese team Porto. Ironically, the Porto team was coached at that time by José Mourinho, who would later lead the Real Madrid soccer team— Barcelona´s arch rival—during some of the most intensely competitive years of Lio´s career.

When Messi joined Barcelona´s first team, Ronaldinho, the Brazilian superstar, was Barcelona´s best player and an international phenomenon. After Messi started training with the first team, however, Ronaldinho admitted to his teammates that he was sure than Messi would go on to become a greater player than he was. In 2006, Ronaldinho was awarded the Ballon D´or for his stellar season, but while accepting the award he said, "This award says I'm the best player in the world, but I´m not even the best player at Barcelona," in reference to Messi.

But Messi didn´t let the praise go to his head. He realized that his lack of size and strength would affect him while playing at the higher level, so he began to dedicate himself to increasing his strength and muscle mass. He was weaker than other opponents who were both taller and stronger than him, but his drive to change that was unshakable.

After months of practicing with the first team, the senior players on Barcelona's first team were so impressed by his ability, drive and determination that they petitioned Coach Frank Rijkaard to give Messi a chance to play during league play.

On October 16th, he finally debuted against the team Espanyol, and at seventeen years, three months and twenty two days old, he became the youngest player to play for Barcelona in an official competition. That record was later broken by Messi's former teammate Bojan Krkic.

His first goal came on May 1st, 2005 against

Albacete and fittingly enough, that goal was assisted by Ronaldinho. It was a symbolic passing of the guard, as Ronaldinho understood that in the near future Messi would become the star of the team. He became, at that time, the youngest player to score for the Barcelona team. That year, Barcelona won the Spanish League for the first time in six years.

During the 2005-2006 season, Messi became a regular starter for Barcelona´s first team, sharing the striker position with Ronaldinho and Samuel Eto´. Together, they formed one of the most lethal trios of forwards in the game at the time. He started in major games like the Classic against Real Madrid, and in the Round of 16 Champions League game against Chelsea.

He had scored 8 goals in 25 games before tearing his hamstring in the return leg of the Champions League Round of 16 against Chelsea. With Barcelona in great form, Messi wanted to recover from his injury in order to support his team if they were to make it to the Champions League Final.

Barcelona did make it to the Champions League Final that year, but on the day of the game, Messi was told that he wasn't medically cleared to play. Barcelona eventually won the Champions League against the English side of Arsenal. Messi was so frustrated that he wasn't able to take the field and help his team that he didn't celebrate his team's win. Though he later apologized, his competitive desire to be on the field at all times further showed his drive to win and become the best player he could be.

During the 2006-2007 season, Barcelona's team gradually began to decline, but Messi was establishing himself as one of the world's best players. He scored 17 goals in 36 games during that season, but two of his goals in particular, stood out.

Diego Maradona was an Argentinean soccer player that played in the 1980's and 1990's; and, along with the Brazilian Pelé, was arguably one of soccer's all time great players. Undoubtedly, he was Argentina's greatest player.

In a span of two weeks during the 2006-2007 season, Messi replicated two of Maradona's most famous goals, the "Goal of the Century" and the "Hand of God" goal. Maradona's "goal of the century" came during the 1986 World Cup, where he took the ball at midfield and dribbled through the entire defense to score an unassisted goal. Messi, in the Copa Del Rey semifinal in 2007, scored a similar goal as he took the ball from 60 yards away and dribbled past at least half the defense before scoring a remarkable goal.

A few weeks later, Messi scored a goal from a "header" with a little help from his hand. As he dove for the ball, his hand helped push the ball past the goalkeeper. Maradona, in the same World Cup game, had scored a similar goal that became known as the "Hand of God."

Maradona admitted in 2008 that, "I have seen the player who will inherit my place in Argentine football and his name is Messi. Messi is a genius, and he can become an even better player. His potential is limitless, and I think he's got everything it takes to become Argentina's greatest player."

But Messi, ever the humble and reserved person, replied in 2010, by saying, "Diego is Diego and for me, he is the greatest player of all time. Even after a million years, I am not even going to be close to Maradona. I have no intention of comparing myself with Maradona. I want to make my own history for something I have achieved."

After Ronaldinho began to lose form during the 2007 season, Messi became the face of the franchise. He was even given the nickname "Messiah" by Barcelona´s fans that recognized his otherworldly abilities.

However, Messi struggled with injuries. Between 2006 and 2008, he missed over 8 months of playing time with different muscular injuries. Some people thought that because of his size, he was overly vulnerable to being injured while playing alongside bigger and stronger opponents. Other people wondered if he would be able to stay in shape long enough to grow into the player he was becoming. With his injury problems, Messi was facing another obstacle that threatened the greatness of his career.

CHAPTER SIX

THE HISTORIC FIRST TREBLE

"I'm lucky to be a part of a team who help to make me look good, and they deserve as much of the credit for my success as I do." – Lionel Messi

AFTER HIS FIRST FEW YEARS on the first team, Barcelona went into a gradual decline. Ronaldinho was no longer the dominant superstar that he once was. Coach Frank Rijkaard was fired and Barcelona had gone two whole seasons without any major trophies.

Messi had battled with injuries over those

two years, and if he was to replace Ronaldinho as the next superstar on Barcelona´s squad, he needed to find a way to stay fit for an entire season. Barcelona hired a personal physiotherapist for Messi and implemented a nutrition and training regime directly tailored to his situation. Messi followed the new regime religiously, which helped him to regain form and maintain his health throughout the course of the year. During the next four years of his career he remained virtually injury free, allowing him to blossom into the world renowned player that he is today.

After the firing of Rijkaard, Barcelona took a chance on a former Barcelona player and captain, Pep Guardiola. Guardiola was a young coach, and his only experience was with the Barcelona B Team. However, the risk paid off as Guardiola quickly established himself as one of the best coaches in modern soccer.

Guardiola had played for Barcelona during

the coaching tenure of Johan Cruyff, the famous Dutch coach known for prioritizing ball control and passing. Once he assumed the reigns of Barcelona's first team, Guardiola quickly implemented the famous "tiki-taka" style of soccer, where Barcelona would play keep away from other opponents for large stretches of time and would almost always dominate the percentage of ball control during the game.

Recognizing that he had something special in Messi, Pep also moved Messi from his normal position and gave him the freedom to roam the field and create opportunities wherever he saw fit. This new independence on the field helped improve and capitalize on Messi's natural play-making ability, and during the 2008-2009 campaign he scored 38 goals in 51 games.

Perhaps one of the greatest moments of that record setting season was when Barcelona travelled to Madrid to play their arch rivals Real Madrid. Messi scored twice and had one assist enroute to a massive 6-2 victory over Real Madrid, the most lop-sided victory of the Classic between the two rival teams.

Barcelona went on to win the Spanish league, the Copa Del Rey and the Champions League during that season. In the Champions League final against Manchester United, Messi's header goal was the final touch on a fantastic season. It was the first time in the history of Spanish soccer that a team won the famous "Treble," winning all three of the major trophies they competed for.

But Barcelona wasn't finished. They finished 2009 with a total of six major trophies, also winning the Spanish Supercopa, the UEFA Super Cup and the FIFA Club World Cup. In the final of the FIFA Club World Cup, Messi scored the winning goal off of his chest. Never before had a team won all six of the major trophies in one calendar year. It was, beyond any shadow of doubt, one of the most memorable seasons in the history of soccer.

As the best player on the best team in the world, Messi easily won the Ballon D'or and the FIFA Player of the Year Award, beating out Real Madrid player Cristiano Ronaldo who had beaten him the previous year. At 22 years old, Messi was one of the youngest players to ever receive these trophies. He also was chosen by the greatest voting margin in the history of both trophies.

CHAPTER SEVEN

A WELL DECORATED STAR

"If football has taught me anything, it is that you can overcome anything if, and only if, you love something enough." – Lionel Messi

AFTER SUCH AN EXPLOSIVE AND record setting season, what else could Messi and his Barcelona teammates accomplish? Coach Pep Guardiola admitted that Messi, "was probably the best player that he had ever seen." Barcelona's board of directors thought the same and rewarded Messi with a massive new contract, one of the largest and most expensive in the world. Part of the contract read that if any other team wanted to buy Messi away from Barcelona, they would have to pay a 250 million Euro fee to Barcelona, thus basically assuring that Messi would stay at Barcelona for years to come. After almost having lost their star when he was a youngster, Barcelona's board of directors didn't want to risk making the same mistake again.

During the next few seasons, Messi continued his brilliance by breaking almost every record in the book. He became the first player in Barcelona history to score two hat tricks in back to back games. In a 2010 Champions League game against Arsenal, he also became the first Barcelona player to score 4 goals in a game. During that same game, he became the Barcelona player with most goals in the Champions League.

Barcelona won the Spanish League title

again in the 2009-2010 season with a record breaking 99 points for the season. The previous record had been set by Real Madrid at 92 points. Messi once again won the Ballon D´or, as well as the Golden Boot and the "Pichichi" award for most goals scored in the Spanish League and in European competitions.

The 2010-2011 season didn´t slow Barcelona or Messi down one bit. Messi went on to score 53 goals during that season as Barcelona again won the Spanish League title and another Champions League crown. In the Champions League title, once again against Manchester United, Messi scored and was named the most valuable player of the final. He received his third straight Ballon D´or title, being elected together with teammates Andrés Iniesta and Xavi Hernandez as the three finalists.

The 2011-2012 season took Messi to new

heights. He scored an unprecedented 73 goals and created 29 assists in all competitions during 2011, making him the single-season top scorer in the history of European soccer, passing a mark set by the German Gerd Muller in 1973. After Messi broke the mark, Muller said, "My record stood for 40 years and now the best player in the world has broken it, and I'm delighted for him. He is an incredible player, gigantic."

Messi also scored 50 goals in the Spanish League that season setting a new record for most goals in a season. He had a hat trick or more in ten games during that calendar year. He went on to break one of his own personal best records by scoring five goals in a Champions League game against the German side Bayern Leverkusen.

At only 24 years of age, Messi became the all time leading scorer for Barcelona, passing the mark set by Cesar Rodriguez at 234 goals.

That record had stood for 57 years, making it all the more unbelievable that Messi could break the record at such a young age.

If all of that wasn't enough, Messi went on to win a record fourth Ballon D'or. He is the only player to ever have won that award four times, and he did it four years in a row.

Despite Messi's success and individual accomplishments, Barcelona gradually fell into a steady decline after four years of dominating European soccer. After having won 14 trophies under that four year period being coached by Guardiola, Barcelona was only able to win the Copa Del Rey in 2012, the least important of the three major tournaments they played in.

People in the media began speaking of a "Messi-dependence" at Barcelona, arguing that Barcelona depended too much on Messi's magic and had lost the ability to function as a team. Their arch rivals, Real Madrid, coached by José Mourinho and led by Portuguese super star Cristiano Ronaldo, gradually gained ground on Barcelona and were able to win the Spanish League trophy in the 2011-2012 season.

Messi helped Barcelona regain the Spanish League title during the 2012-2013 season under new coach Tita Villanova, his old coach from his days at Barcelona's youth academy. However, after four injury free seasons, Messi again began having problems with injuries. During the Champions League of 2013, Messi was injured but came off the bench to carry his team past AC Milan and Paris Saint Germain, before eventually falling to Bayern Munich in the semifinals.

In November of 2013, Messi tore a hamstring that sidelined him for two months. His production declined once he returned and many people began to predict that the best years of Messi's career were behind him. Barcelona suffered through another season without any trophies during the 2013-2014 schedule.

Rumors began to fly once again concerning Messi's future at Barcelona. Various clubs from around Europe made offers for Messi, but despite the speculation and uncertainty, Lio eventually signed a record setting contract with Barcelona, making him the highest paid player in soccer. Despite his massive contract, Messi maintained, "Money is not a motivating factor. Money doesn't thrill me or make me play better because there are benefits to being wealthy. I'm just happy with a ball at my feet. My motivation comes from playing the game I love. If I wasn't paid to be a professional footballer I would willingly play for nothing."

In 2015, Barcelona hired another former player as their new head coach. Luis Enrique was famous for his versatility during his days as a player, having played in almost every position on the pitch. He promised to return Barcelona to the brilliance that it had enjoyed in previous seasons.

Messi began the season in great form, finally injury free. In November of 2014 he surpassed Telmo Zarra for the most goals scored in the Spanish League. Zarra's record had stood for more than 59 years. Messi, only 26 at the time, will surely continue to add to his total making the new record almost unbreakable in the future.

Three days after breaking the record for most goals in the Spanish League, he scored a hat trick to become the highest scoring player of all time in the Champions League. He passed a record set by former Real Madrid player, Raul.

Despite getting off to a fast start under new coach Luis Enrique, Barcelona soon started digging themselves a rut. During one particularly disappointing loss, Luis Enrique made the decision to sit Messi. The media brought up rumors of tension between Messi and his coach, and as they fell further behind Real Madrid in the standings, some wondered if Messi would be leaving the club for real this time.

But as the season began to wind toward a close, Messi, together with Neymar and Luis Suarez, joined together to become one of the most feared attacking trios in the game. Suarez had joined Barcelona during the off season, and after serving a 3 month ban for having bitten an opponent during the World Cup, he quickly found his rhythm alongside Messi and Neymar.

Those three, deemed MSN for their initials, finished the season with 122 goals between the three of them. Messi contributed 58, but it became obvious that in Neymar and Suarez,

Barcelona had found a way to free itself from its supposed "Messi-dependence."

Barcelona finished the year in top fashion, winning the Spanish League Title, the Copa Del Rey and the Champions League. They thus became the only team to ever win two "Trebles." Messi was fundamental in the Champions League for Barcelona, leading Barcelona to a fantastic win over Bayern Munich in the semi-finals, the same side that had embarrassed them two years before and that was now coached by Pep Guardiola. In the final against the Italian side Juventus, Messi participated in all three of Barcelona's goals. Messi was awarded his fifth Ballon D'or in 2015, adding to his record for most Ballon D'or in the history of the sport.

CHAPTER EIGHT

THE QUEST FOR THE WORLD CUP

"Goals are only important if they win games." – Lionel Messi

MESSI'S SUCCESS ON A CLUB level is undisputed. No other player can claim the same amount of individual and team success. He has taken Barcelona to the height of the soccer world and is recognized as one of the greatest, if not the greatest, player in the world.

But on a national team level, success hasn't

come as easy. A number of critics have questioned why Messi has won so many trophies for Barcelona, but none for his home country of Argentina. Some go so far as to say that Messi is only the player that he is because of the fact that he is surrounded by such great talent at Barcelona. Having Xavi Hernandez and Andrés Iniesta as midfielders to set him up with great passes is what contributes to his individual success, they argue, and without those playmakers behind him he is not the same player. Others claim that he cares more about his club than his country.

Messi is a dual citizen of Argentina and Spain and could have chosen to play for either country. Despite being recruited by the Spanish National Team, he chose to represent his home country of Argentina.

Messi joined the Argentina National team in 2004 at the age of 17. In 2005, he helped the Argentina youth squad win the World Youth

Championship, beating Brazil (the defending champions) in the semifinals and Nigeria in the final. He finished as the tournament's top scorer.

Later in 2005 he debuted on Argentina's first national team in a friendly match against Hungary. He came on as a substitute in the second half and was sent off with a red card two minutes later after a questionable call by the referee. Messi was so distraught over being sent off during his international debut that he was found crying in the locker room after the game.

His first goal with the Argentina national team came against Croatia in March of 2006. In the 2006 World Cup, he became the youngest player to ever take the field for Argentina and the youngest Argentinean to score in the World Cup. In the quarter finals against Germany, Argentina's national coach, José Pekerman, opted to leave Messi on the bench. Barcelona lost 4-2 in a penalty shootout, and Pekerman was widely criticized for not having played Messi.

During the 2008 Olympic Games, Messi was initially prohibited from playing by Barcelona. However, new coach Pep Guardiola intervened on Messi´s behalf, allowing him to play. After beating Brazil in the semi-finals, Argentina went on to beat Nigeria to become the Olympic gold medal winners.

Diego Maradona, Argentina´s most famous player (besides Messi, perhaps) took over as head coach of the Argentina National Team in 2008. Though they struggled in the qualifying rounds, they eventually found their form during the 2010 World Cup. Messi helped coach Maradona devise a strategy that placed him behind two other strikers. The strategy worked well during the beginning of the World Cup as Argentina easily won its group.

But in the quarter finals Argentina was again defeated by Germany, by a score of 4-0.

Argentina had last won a World Cup in 1986 with Maradona leading the team. After 28 years, Argentina was getting impatient. After all, they had one of the best players in the world in Messi, and a star-studded support cast surrounding him. The 2014 World Cup was supposed to be Argentina's time to shine.

Messi limped into the World Cup after an injury plagued season at Barcelona. However, he quickly regained his form as he carried his team through the group stage. He was named "man of the match" for the first four games he played, and almost single-handedly led his team to consecutive victories over Bosnia and Herzegovina, Iran and Nigeria.

In the Round of 16, Lio provided a crucial assist in a win over Switzerland before helping to set up the only goal of the match in a 1-0 victory over Belgium in the quarter finals. After beating the Netherlands in a penalty shootout in the semifinals, Argentina advanced to the finals to face Germany, the same team that had knocked them out in the previous two World Cups. It was also a rematch of the 1990 World Cup Final.

Messi played well but missed various opportunities for the game winning goal. He set up a beautiful pass to teammate Gonzalo Higuain whose goal was questionably considered off sides by the referee. Germany eventually scored in extra time sending Argentina to a heart breaking defeat. Messi was elected the best player of the tournament, though that award was bitter sweet after finishing runner up to Germany. He finished the tournament with 4 goals, one assist and as the player to have created the most opportunities for goals.

The loss in the World Cup, and another loss

in the finals of the Copa de America a year later, brought criticism to the Argentina national team and to Messi in particular. Despite his success at Barcelona, many people believed that in order to secure his legacy as the world's best player, he needed to win a major tournament for his country, preferably the World Cup.

When the 2018 World Cup comes around, Messi will be 31 years old, and that will likely be his last chance to win the World Cup for his country. In order to silence the critics who claim that he is the best club player, yet not the best all around player in the history of the game, Lio will have to try and carry his country to the long awaited World Cup Championship. Lio has said, "I want to be world champion, but not to change the perception of others towards me or to achieve greatness like they say, but rather to reach the goal with my national team and to add a world cup to my list of titles."

Responding to his critics that say that he loves his club more than his country, Lio has said, "I've never stopped being Argentinean, and I've never wanted to. I feel very proud of being Argentine, even though I left there. I've been clear about this since I was very young, and I never wanted to change. Barcelona is my home because both the club and the people here have given me everything, but I won't stop being Argentine.

CHAPTER NINE

MESSI OFF THE FIELD

"I try to do my bit to make people's lives more bearable, in particular children across the globe who are having problems." – Lionel Messi

SAMUEL ETO', ONE OF LIO Messi's former teammates, once said, "Messi is a God, as a person and even more as a player." While watching Messi play, it is all too easy to forget that he has a life off the field. While watching highlight after highlight of his record setting goals, we tend to forget that he is also a father to two young children, a boyfriend to his long-time girlfriend, a son, a brother, and so many other things.

Messi has maintained a relationship with his girlfriend, Antonella Rocuzzo, since 2008. He has known Antonella since the time he was five years old, as both of them grew up together in his native town of Rosario in Argentina. In 2012, Messi's first son, Thiago, was born. Soon after his first son's birth, Messi declared on his Twitter account, "Today I am the happiest man in the world, my son was born and thanks to God for this gift." In 2015, Mateo, Messi's second son, was born and Messi said, "Being a dad changes everything for the better and I'm really enjoying it."

He has also said that being a father has changed his perspective on his professional soccer career. According to Lio, being a father "...has also changed the way I see a match. Before, if I lost or did something wrong, I didn't talk to anyone for three or four days, until it passed. Now, I come home after a game, I see my son and everything is alright." The experience of being a father hasn't diminished Lio's competitive spirit, but it has helped him to see that there are other, more important aspects to life.

Lio maintains a very close relationship with his family as well. He has a tattoo of his mother on his left shoulder, as well as a tattoo of his first son on his calf. His father is his professional agent, while one of his brothers is his publicist.

Lio has also been very involved in a number of charitable activities. His own medical issues as a child were a stimulus to help him put children's rights as a priority for the charitable work he is involved in. The Lio Messi foundation was founded by Messi and his family in 2007 and focuses on working with children around the world.

The foundation was developed by Lio in order to help young people around the world create new opportunities to achieve their dreams and aspirations. Lio´s mother Celia helps manage the foundation. Access to health and education are the two main centers of action of the foundation, though it also helps develop sporting initiatives for young people around the world.

Lio explains, "One day, after a visit to a hospital, I understood the special dimension of a public figure. I understood that for those sick children, the presence of a famous soccer player can be helpful. You stand there and you give away your smile and you understand that for them that is a special joy, because they have to keep fighting in order to overcome their disease and pursue their dreams."

Messi´s visit to that Boston hospital for terminally ill children in 2007 led him to the decision that he needed to invest part of his earnings into some worthwhile humanitarian cause.

Lio goes on to explain, "I reached my dream of becoming a soccer player and I want (all the children) to know that I fought hard to get where I am, and I have to fight even harder to keep my dreams intact. I want to use my success to help children who need it most. I am excited every day when I get a child to smile and when he thinks that there is hope. For this reason we decided to create the Leo Messi Foundation, and I will keep fighting to make children happy with the same energy that I fight to maintain myself a successful soccer player."

Part of the funding for his foundation comes from the "Lio and friends" soccer matches that he organizes. These friendly soccer games pair Messi with other world-renowned soccer players, and the funds raised go to help his foundation support medical projects around the world.

Lio was also named Goodwill Ambassador to UNICEF, the United Nations Children's Fund, in 2010. As Ambassador, Messi is expected to use his fame to draw attention to important issues that children face around the world. In 2010, shortly after assuming his role as goodwill ambassador, Messi traveled to Haiti to advocate for children affected by the devastating earthquake that caused hundreds of thousands of casualties. Messi has also participated in campaigns led by UNICEF to stimulate HIV prevention, education, and the inclusion of disabled children.

Messi also maintains a close connection to his hometown of Rosario. Despite having lived in Spain since he was a child, he still maintains his traditional Rosarian accent. Lio currently supports a football club in the neighborhood of Rosario where he was born and grew up.

Since he received so much support during his own youth career, he also funds the management of many young soccer players from Argentina who show promise and talent. Some of those younger players play for Newell's Old Boys, his old club in Rosario. At the installations of Newell's Old Boys, Messi also helped to rebuild some of their infrastructure to improve the conditions for training and practice.

Messi is much more than just a soccer player; he is also a caring and compassionate person who has learned from his own trials, the need to live in solidarity with those less fortunate among us.

CHAPTER TEN

THE KEYS TO MESSI´S SUCCESS

"I start early and I stay late, day after day after day, year after year. It took me 17 years and 114 days to become an overnight success." – Lionel Messi

FOR MANY, LIO MESSI IS by far the best player to have ever stepped onto a soccer field. But in order to get to where he is today, Messi had to overcome numerous obstacles and setbacks. He had to sacrifice the familiarity of life in his hometown, and endure the separation from his family. Once in Barcelona, he had to deal with loneliness and the difficulty of adapting to a new place and routine. During his career, his injuries have caused moments of doubt and tension with his supporters, and clashes with new coaches have also occurred.

In some ways, his success has also been a challenge as well. The international media almost expects him to win every game, every trophy and every award. During the 2013-2014 season, even though Messi still scored 41 goals, Barcelona finished the season without a trophy and the media lost no time in declaring that Messi was finished.

But one aspect that most defines Messi's character, and has been a key to his success, is his ability to avoid the media hype and speculation, and focus on his own drive to continually get better. Despite temporary setbacks, Messi has continually stated, "I prefer to win titles with the team ahead of individual awards, or scoring more goals than anyone else. I'm more worried about being a good person than being the best football player in the world. When all this is over, what are you left with? When I retire, I hope I am remembered for being a decent guy."

Messi has also been able to turn his supposed weaknesses into his strengths. Growing up, he was considered by many as too small to be a world class soccer player. His critics maintained that bigger and stronger defenders would be able to push him off the ball and intimidate him physically.

Messi didn't heed his critics, however, and turned his small stature into one of his greatest assets. His small stature gives him more agility and quickness, and his lower center of gravity allows him to avoid defenders.

He has developed himself as one of the

greatest dribblers of all time. His former coach, Pep Guardiola, once remarked, "Messi is the only player that runs faster with the ball than he does without it." Others marvel at his ability to keep the ball glued to his feet. Maradona once marveled, "The ball stays glued to his foot. I've seen great players in my career, but I've never seen anyone with Messi's ball control."

Angel Di Maria, his opponent that for many years played at Real Madrid, remarked, "Having him as a rival is complicated. You see game after game that it is impossible to take the ball off him, impossible to stop him." Messi also worked hard to develop the upper body strength needed to ward off defenders. He can not only dribble around players, but he can also dribble through defenders.

Perhaps one of the most important keys to Messi's success is his unselfishness. After having won five Ballon D'or, four Champions

League Trophies, seven Spanish League trophies, three Copa de Rey trophies and countless other individual accomplishments, Messi still maintains that his success comes because he is a part of a team that supports him and makes him better. He is the ultimate team player that always puts the team ahead of his own individual accomplishments.

Messi is often compared to Cristiano Ronaldo, the Real Madrid forward whose rivalry with Messi had become legendary. Many consider Messi and Ronaldo to be competing for "best in the world" status, and the fact that the last eight Ballon D´or have been won by either Messi or Ronaldo seems to confirm that idea.

But Messi and Ronaldo are different types of players. Whereas Messi is the ultimate team player, Ronaldo is the ultra-competitive style of player that often times seems to focus more on his own individual achievements. In a 2016 loss to their cross-town rivals Athletic Madrid, Ronaldo claimed that his teammates, "...were not up to his level." Messi responded a few days later with a typical remark of his stating that his success, "...came because of the close knit relations among his teammates; that was the secret of their success."

Messi once remarked that, "It doesn't matter if I am better than Cristiano Ronaldo, all that matters is that Barcelona is better than Madrid." His current teammate, the Turkish international Arda Turan, responded to the most famous question in soccer this way, "Messi or Ronaldo best player in the world? In the world, I would say Ronaldo. Messi is from another planet."

Other famous and important players, both former and current, have spoken about Messi's greatness. Messi commands almost universal respect from the soccer world, and almost all players and coaches agree that there has rarely been a player with his unique skill set.

Former teammate David Villa, the Spanish team's leading all time scorer, says that, "Messi is so talented that 70% of the goals I scored at Barca came from his boots. With him on your team, you're calm."

Villa's comments show that Messi, despite being a great goal scorer, is above all else, a team player with a great vision for the game. Messi is the designated penalty kick specialist for Barcelona's team, but often times he lets other players who are struggling take the penalties in order to get on the scoring sheet. In fact, in a 2016 game, instead of shooting the penalty, Messi actually made a pass from the penalty mark to teammate Luis Suarez who scored off of the penalty "pass."

Mario Gotze was the German player who scored the winning goal against Barcelona in extra time during the 2014 World Cup. Yet, despite being the player that handed Messi one of the worst defeats of his career, Gotze admitted that Messi has "achieved so many great things and set the bar so high that practically nobody is ever going to reach it."

During Barcelona's 2015 run to the Champions League Final, Messi scored one of the most memorable goals of his career against Bayern Munich in the semifinals. He ran past two defenders and then crossed over defender Jerome Boateng, making him fall to the ground before chipping the ball over goal keeper Manuel Neuer. The video of Messi making Boateng fall over became viral on the internet, but Boateng humbly recognized Messi's brilliance. In a 2015 interview he said, "For me, Messi is the best player in the world. Defending Messi one-on-one is not possible."

Gary Lineker was a forward that played in England during the 1980's and was recognized as one of the best strikers of his generation. He was also the maximum scorer during the 1986 World Cup. Despite having an exceptional career of his own, Lineker confessed that, "Messi produces more pieces of exceptional skill in a single game than I managed in an entire career." Even when compared to other great players of soccer history, Messi clearly stands apart in a league of his own.

Messi is obviously one of the most skilled players on the planet, but what has allowed him to morph into a global phenomenon is his soccer IQ. Former teammate Carles Puyol says, "There's a special part of Messi's brain allowing him to see the split-second chaos of football in his own personal super slow motion."

Often times during games, Messi makes miraculous pinpoint passes. He seems to know exactly where the defense is going to be and how to find a way through a wall of ten defenders. Even when he is marked by 2 or 3 defenders, his game is not diminished or slowed. He is one of the most accurate passers on one of history's greatest passing teams, and his football intelligence combines with his unique skill set to create the all around player that he has become.

Paul Scholes, one of the greatest holding midfielders in the history of the English Premier League, perhaps expressed what most of Messi's opponents have felt one time or another, "I am not ashamed to admit that in the games against Barcelona, I spent a lot of the time just hoping Messi would take up positions as far away from me as possible."

CHAPTER ELEVEN

CONCLUSIONS

"I always thought I wanted to play professionally, and I always knew that to do that I'd have to make a lot of sacrifices. I made sacrifices by leaving Argentina, leaving my family to start a new life. I changed my friends, my people. Everything. But everything I did, I did for football, to achieve my dream. – Lionel Messi

THE MAGAZINE ESQUIVEL ONCE DECLARED that "Messi saved football (soccer). There has never been such an overwhelming, devastating, decisive and unique player." Messi has undoubtedly brought a new level of excitement and thrill to soccer. Even the casual observer can tell that when Messi is on the field the game takes on a new intensity and meaning.

The media have run out of adjectives to describe Messi's brilliance. Barney Ronay of the English newspaper, The Guardian, tried to explain Messi's talent this way, "At the Camp Nou, Messi scored two brilliant goals, made a third and at times yawned his way around champion opponents like a man tactfully avoiding a gaggle of overheated toddlers in a high street coffee shop. Often, he took the ball and shimmied past two or three men, operating within a kind of fermata, events slowed and paused around him, and providing a reminder that he remains one of the great dribblers, master of the flip-flap, the surge, the amphetamine-crazed-millipede shift of feet."

Graham Hunter, a reporter for ESPN,

considers that when Messi is on the field, "It's like watching raging bulls. He's got extraordinary strength for a small man. Yet, he'll score goals, as if they're going out of fashion. Nobody's ever scored goals at this ratio."

But Messi has never let the admiration and praise of the media go to his head. What is so fascinating and captivating about Messi, is that despite his success, he still takes to the field every game as if he were 10 years old and playing at Newell's Old Boys club in Argentina. Messi simply loves to play soccer, and though the records come and the contracts and the individual and team awards rain upon him, the most important aspect of the game for him is simply being on the field and having the ball at his feet.

Messi has said that, "The only thing that matters is playing. I have enjoyed it since I was a little boy and I still try to do that every time

I go out onto a pitch. I always say that when I no longer enjoy it or it's no longer fun to do it, then I won't do it anymore. I do it because I love it and that's all I care about. To be honest, at that moment [when my contract was signed on that napkin], I never would have dreamed that this would happen to me. I never could have imagined that I was going to live the life that I have. I'd always dreamed of being a top football player and I'm living my dream."

But as we've seen, Messi's success hasn't come easily. He is not simply a supernaturally gifted soccer player, but rather his success has come from a lifetime of sacrifice, hard work and dedication.

From the time that he first took to the pitch as a four year old, undersized child accompanied by his grandmother, all the way to his record fifth Ballon D'or trophy, Messi has worked hard to achieve his dream of becoming the best soccer player of all time.

At only 28 years old, Messi is far from finished. He still has at least another 4 or 5 years of quality football left. He will undoubtedly add to his goal scoring record in both the Champions League and the Spanish League, records that will likely stand for many years to come.

He may very well lead Barcelona to another Champions League title, to more Spanish League trophies, and perhaps even to an unprecedented third (or fourth) Treble. And, on a national level, perhaps 2018 will be the year that Messi guides Argentina to the long awaited World Cup Title.

It is a rarity to come across players like Lionel Messi, those who combine supernatural skill with a heartfelt love for the game. Messi´s former coach, Pep Guardiola, said it best when he advised, "Don't write about him...don't try to describe him. Just watch him." Let´s hope that we can continue to enjoy watching Messi for years to come.

Made in the USA
San Bernardino, CA
14 January 2017